THE GHOST NET

THE GHOST NET

ALAN JENKINS

NEW WALK EDITIONS
Leicester & Nottingham

In memory of Marie Colvin (1956-2012)
and Hugh Hudson (1936-2023)

Published by New Walk Editions
c/o Rory Waterman
Department of English, Philosophy and Linguistics,
Nottingham Trent University, NG11 8NS
and
c/o Nick Everett, Centre for New Writing,
University of Leicester, LE1 7RH

www.newwalkmagazine.com

Printed by imprintdigital, Upton Pyne, Exeter.

Contents

A Song of Maine   9
B&B   10
Look-out   12
Between   13
Master and Commander   14
Salt-water Days   15
Deptford   24
Sailor, Adrift   27
To the Lighthouse: Finistère   28
Spray   30
Shark Song   32
Free Enterprise   34
Feeder   35
A Night Sail   36
Ledbury Road   44
Between (Reprise)   45
Night-swimming, Regent's Park   48
Inshore   49
Sirens' Song   52
Poster Girl   53
At Richmond   54
Salvage
    Heroes   56
    Back Numbers   56
    Personal   57
    Mr Crabtree Goes Fishing   57
    London Irish   58
    Duffel Coat   58
    Clipper   59
Smoke   60
In Sailor's Locker   62
Player's Navy   63
John Knox Laughton in West Kensington   64
Blue Days (Sailor's Return)   67
Notes and Acknowledgements   76

A Song of Maine

It seemed absurd,
To be flying up to Maine,
An 'honoured guest', the week I'd heard
That my life would never be the same again,
That the time had come to pay for every word
I'd let go in unkindness, or in haste,
Every chance I'd let go to waste,
Each drag, each drunken fuck,
Each drop of booze,
Each bit of undeserved good luck
I'd somehow refused to use;

That I who'd been
The doctor, was now the disease…
Could I have known, could I have seen
How I'd mislay that knack I had, to please
By a sort of laying on of hands?
Or, now that I had lost my touch
So that a single touch of mine appalled,
And everything came down to cells and glands,
How much, how much
I'd need you, or that when you called
To say *I wasn't real*, what that would mean?

I sat and stared
At the grey Atlantic, at
The grey mist that rolled unimpaired
Over pines and firs, grey rock and where I sat –
A granite perch on Schooner Head, a deck I shared
With foxes, squirrels and a grey raccoon
– Its mask of sadness; at the moon,
Most nights, as it sailed through
A storm-rinsed sky
To mock me and my need for you,
Absurd as that seemed, to its eye.

B&B

I knew the path, the promenade, the lanes,
The park where a stone Victoria frowned
At lichen-covered benches, salt insistent rains
(I could have lost myself, I could have drowned),
The rust-streaked wet clay of the undercliff;
Heaps of rotted feathers, stinking bladderwrack,
Gull-shit and tar-stains, and the intimate whiff
In broken shells. Why had I come back?

I knew the path they called the Coastal Walk –
A sheer drop to hissing shingle, and the slosh
Of foaming breakers, spindrift, backwash,
The jagged rocks and eddies under talk
Of what we'd eat (some pricey fish-based gunk);
Farther out, the sliced-off, rust-gripped hulls
Of wrecked merchantmen, and wind-flung gulls –
Drowned sailor-souls. . . Every evening, sunk

In silence, clenched tight as mussels and half-pissed,
We took unsteady steps down to the 'beach'
(*How her muscles clenched tight on you!*): through mist,
A harbour-pastoral of masts just out of reach;
Lamps festooned the 'Captain's Cabin', nets, so much
Old rope – and there it started, nights of Please,
It's not a good time. Of Look but don't touch,
Of your look that brought me to my knees!

(In cooling bathwater, in a stench of fish
And mildew, I groped for the sliver of soap
That slid from the B&B's scallop-shell dish –
Grey suds slopped overboard. . . And did I hope
To see you now, pale skin, pale pubic blur
As you peeled off your one-piece? *Could she tell –*
How much you'd miss the feel of scallop-shell
Slippiness inside; that you'd be back for her?)

I knew the path across sand-dunes and rocks
To a concrete pillbox: piss-and-damp-mould smell,
Charred driftwood, condoms like the ghosts of cocks;
Outside, the washing of the channel swell
Through winding culverts to a weed-fringed pool
Where sea-anemone and scuttling crab
Shrank from my groping fingers and a school
Of gobies darted, when I knelt once to grab –

Only a white sea-smoothed pebble in my hand,
The crab had vanished in a cloudy swirl.
A brisk rub-down, the towel stiff with sand
And salt – aged nine, I watched a little girl,
Wet cotton clinging to her sun-browned skin
As she ran shrieking in the shallows' sudsy foam,
Ran shrieking back: *I'm going in!* –
A last-swim sadness, last day before home. . .

Don't touch, don't touch: the tightly puckered bud,
The fronds that wave like underwater hair,
The yellow froth that comes in with the flood,
The pale gooseflesh in salt astringent air. . .
I'd never find our windbreak that was hung
With leathery strands of sea-kelp, or peer
Through stinging lashes at wet cloth where it clung
To you when you climbed ahead of me up here –

The narrow track, zig-zag that clings to chalk;
Above me, slate-grey sky, a flapping flag
Torn from an old Red Ensign, and the squawk
Of gulls that bobbed around that fraying rag,
Its empire shrunk to this, a cliff, a path
That led me winding back where I'd come from –
A mildewed B&B, a bar, a bath –
Through spray the wind whipped up above the prom.

Look-out

I know the path (and what a new kind of hurt
It is, this trying not to remember)
Across the marsh to dunes and marram grass,

To the sea, to miles of sand at Camber
Where she waded in, laughing, with her skirt
Tucked up somehow around her thighs and arse…

From our room the sea was a guessed-at blur –
Our top-floor room, 'The Crow's Nest', where she asked,
Do you want to wrestle? and I came to grips with her,

Her thighs, her hips. I know the underpass,
The First-Aid hut and lifeguards' look-out post
(*First-aid or lifeguard, which do you need most?*),

Small boats pulling off-white wrinkled threads
In the grey silk of the sea; a sharp stink like the heads
In our old Thames-side HQ. *Same old riff:*

What if   What if   What if   What if   What if…
I know the sea-wall, the little stagnant lough,
The high-stepping waders' curving strand.

Gull-cries follow me towards the point, cut off
On three sides, where I have to take myself in hand
As that wave breaks over me, goes back out

And leaves me beached and retching for air
And sea and sky and solid ground in doubt –
Wading in, skirt bunched, laughing: *She is not there.*

Between

Some time between *Plenty* and *Betrayal*,
Between Kate Nelligan in a black,
Waisted plunge-line '50s dress
Looking me straight in the eye
When she took her bow, and the back
Of Penelope Wilton's mini-skirt,
As 'Jerry' clutched her arse,
Riding up dangerously high;

Between my last pair of denim
Hipster flares and my first
Pair of corduroy Oxford bags,
Between wanting to be taken for
The standard hippy-Fauntleroy
And the lost *Picture Post* boy
Who'd spat some lyrical venom
And died in the Spanish Civil War;

Between 'Night Fever' and 'Some Girls',
Between a monkish book-lined cell
And a bijou flat in Battersea
Paid for by the invisible Man,
Between my last-ever Mandrax
And my first line of coke (I'd gone
Straight to drug heaven from drug hell),
Between invasion and peace plan;

Between a life I'd counted on
And the end of that self-flattery:
You were born, whom I met over *kirs*
Thirty years later. Between first kiss
And last, between offering your tail,
Your mobile number and email address
And administering the *coup de grâce*,
You brought me to my knees. To this.

Master and Commander

It was projected on a white sheet like a sail
That billowed gently in the warm night air, remember?
That summer's big hit in England, it couldn't fail
To be the main event out there, in late September.

For two hours, lost in the great three-master's
Plunging and rolling, I roared out my commands.
I was the most masterful of masters,
I boarded you to the cheering of all hands.

'Lads, I give you the *Sophie!*' The Greek sky applauded,
Lit a billion stars as through cannon-smoke that blew
Around me and a hail of shot, I forded
Rivers of fallen men and hacked my way to you.

But something disarmed me, and I lost my prize,
Surrendered it, rather…Where are you sleeping,
Tonight, far from that little open-air cinema, and me,
No more the wise commander, compassionate, proud,

But the midshipman with blond curls who closes his friend's eyes
And, one-handed, sews up the canvas shroud,
The blanched and bloodstained body they commit to the sea,
And the coward with his grog bottle in the fo'c'sle, weeping?

Salt-water Days

There's greenhorn fellows, some on board
Before ne'er saw salt water;
When come to sea, upon my word,
The case with them does alter.
There are snotty boys of midshipmen,
Haven't yet done shitting yellow;
As to their age, some hardly ten
Strike many a brave fellow.

Old sailors' song

The little cruiser chugged past Faversham, upstream on the Swale;
Diesel, bilge and backwash and the reek of adolescent male
Filled the wheelhouse as I ran her shattered bows into the shale.

'*Hurrumph!*' The tannoy screeched and rasped and spluttered into life
And from it came a voice I knew: 'Get it cut, boy, or – or – or –'
(He grabbed a hank of my hair): '*Or give me that sail-knife!*'

That long-dead master-mariner! So hugely-eared
He could have gull-winged down the rope-hung corridor,
Who growled his orders through a nicotine-striated beard

And barked at us through yellowed teeth clenched on his pipe
Now scowled at me and grunted from the after-cabin door,
'*Make all this ship-shape!* I've got your measure, boy, I know your type:

I've seen you hoist a tattered sail
And jib and tack and navigate
Among the shoals and sheltered moles
Owned by the drinking classes,
In the stews of Notting Dale,
In Portobello's narrow strait;
I've seen you search midshipmen's souls
While eyeing up their pretty arses.

I've seen you come about and heave to
In the chill of early morning
(As you used to do, a motley crew,
In Surrey Docks when day was dawning)
After shipping grog with Mick, the bo'sun,
And O'Brien the second mate;
After trying tricks you learnt in Chosun
Down below with Beth or Kate. . .

You signed up for rum, bum and the lash, Southampton to Lahore
But you heard the south sing o'er the land at Fairlight and at Ore
So you affected Oxford bags, the elbow-patches pansies wore

And learned to lisp in numbers. Now your daemon has been trapped;
The time-wasting, skirt-chasing years when nothing scanned,
Everything you are and care for standing ready to be scrapped

Like *Ark Royal* and half the fleet…The sea-roads not taken!
The shadows on the wave-ridged, gull-flecked, glistening sand;
The captains and the deckhands and the quiet berths forsaken.

Remember summer evenings with that stink at ebb and flood –
Not of post-match changing rooms, stale jockstraps and stale socks
But rotting gulls and fish-heads on the bottle-sprouting mud

Where treasure-twitchers picked through tidal leavings, pungent silt? –
The sewer-sump that was the Thames, its bilge-collecting docks;
The sickly green at waterline, froth that factories had spilt…?

Remember Southwark dawn-mist clearing,
Bare-knuckle fights, the knocks and shocks
You took behind the boating sheds?
Remember when those big pressed men,
Your shipmates, grabbed their cocks
And tossed themselves off, leering,
To your cheering in the heads?
Then made you toss them off again…

How a slight swell left you queasy?
Your indecision on the poop?
The captain in cahoots with half the crew
Aboard that ship of fools, your little sloop…
The harbour at Rangoon! The great Zambesi!
True north, Trafalgar, circumnavigation –
These might have made a man of you!
Your birthright and your nation!'

Then he faded, with the shore where he'd tarnished at quiet anchor,
With the wharves and sheds, the rigs and derricks and the tanker
He had captained, and my 'shipmates' shouting *Wanker!*...

~~~

When I came to Greenwich town
There were lasses plenty;
I boldly steppèd up to one
To court her for her beauty.
I said 'My dear, be of good cheer
I will not leave, you need not fear.
I will travel the country through and through
And still be a rambling sailor.'

The voices in my head that talk
Were talking now. This was the walk
Of shame, a boozy saunter down
A certain creek not far from town –
A brackish reach off Greenwich Park,
The silhouetted *Cutty Sark* –
And I heard whispers far below
The river's susurrating flow.

'*Too late!*. . .To sign on, take the helm,
To master that unruly realm
Your father loved, who often sat
With Conrad, Forester, Marryat,
With tales of HMS *Kelly* or
The *Compass Rose*; who kept a store
Of ships' gear salvaged here and there –
Deck-cleats, a binnacle, a pair

Of pulley-blocks – up in his den
And took them out to show you when
You pleaded with him. Too late now,
To steer for home and show him how
Your hard-learned seamanship had brought
Three stripes, a wife in every port –
Not even one wife, and no son
Or daughter shares your setting sun.

Too late to hear the hue and cry
That pierces through a slate-grey sky
As gale-defying gulls go wheeling
Round you on the deck, head reeling:
You let that life go, and instead
Pursued the plunder found in bed,
A woman's love, or else desire –
Your bridges burnt, your boats on fire.'

(A beer-sluiced alley by the pub,
The slime-dark steps, the rowing-club –
One night, the wind still in my sail
I grabbed a mermaid by the tail
And learnt her salty parts of speech,
A tongue that only she could teach;
That barmaid who with practised hand
Pumped up a storm here on dry land. . .)

'Too late to go back now, to him
With pipe and whisky and *Lord Jim*,
To her with plates of food and smiles
For all – a mother's harmless wiles;
Too late for you to talk, to plumb
Those depths you kept forever mum
About, the lives off-course, the lie
And how she had enraged you by

Allowing him to drift, to drown
In sight of her unhappy frown –
She, locked in fear; he, so far gone
By supper time, the TV on,
That snoring shook his "snoozing chair" –
You might as well not have been there.
The hurt and harm you did each other! –
Self-absorbed son, doting mother. . .

Too late to talk, to clear the air,
To make a clean breast, to declare
The home they made a living hell;
Too late to feel the ocean swell
Or take the plunge, to tie the knot,
To leave off roving, stop the rot,
To marry and bring joy to her:
Instead you stayed a boy to her!'

A boat reduced to ribs and keel,
A fridge, a pram with one bent wheel
Had washed up with me on this reach,
A narrow condom-littered beach;
A stray dog loped and picked among
The flotsam, and flicked out a tongue
To lap the yellow seepage, calm
In storm-drains, and my offered palm.

~~~

Why should we here our time delay
In London void of pleasure?
Let's haste away to Brighton Bay
And ransack there for treasure.
Here we must creep and play bo-peep
To shun the damned press-masters;
We live in strife, even die in life,
Confined by catchpole bastards. . .

The shore had long dissolved in mist, though I could still see, faint
As a work in pen-and-wash, a kind of painting without paint,
And hear – the sound a salt sea makes in landlocked long complaint –

The broken pier, the rock-pools full of gear and bobbing skulls,
The slap of rotting fish and fear around the rusted hulls;
The shouts of young men on the beer, the shrieks of half-mad gulls.

'How long since you were here? Since that last time, when you sat
On a slow train that meandered through the south-east, stopping at
Each washed-up last resort and seaside suburb bright with tat?'

I knew this voice, its joshing pedantry, its kindly tone
Of mild amusement at some joke perceived by him alone,
Masking – disappointment? Love? (One I once took for my own…)

'You will always come back, now, wherever you may rove'
(It was true, I seemed to know this coast, its every creek and cove
From Portland Bill to Beachy Head by way of Rye and Hove)

' – Where I retired, a cut-price Prufrock, to walk upon the beach,
Imagining I heard the mermaids singing, each to each;
Saying to the air those lines it fell to me to "teach". . .

Remember me now? It was my battered Penguin Rimbaud
That you stuffed in your backpack when you boarded, years ago,
The Dover-Calais ferry; that you took out down below!'

My sad heart slobbers on the poop,
My heart all black-tobacco-blue;
They chuck at it their gobs of gloop,
My sad heart slobbering on the poop –
Under the piss-taking of this crew
Who laugh themselves to death it's true
My sad heart slobbers on the poop,
My heart all black-tobacco-blue.

Ithyphallic, squaddie-like
Their pissy little jokes have fucked it.
In the wheelhouse, carved with a spike
They left the legend, squaddie-like:
'Jenkins loves my cock, and sucked it'.
Abracadabra! Waves, conduct it
To be washed (my heart, I mean); it's like,
Their pissy little jokes have fucked it.

When they have chewed their baccy dry
What shall we do, my heart, old shag?
There'll be Bacchic hiccups by and by
When they have chewed their baccy dry;
I'll heave up my guts, sky-high,
Me, if it doesn't make them gag.
When they have chewed their baccy dry,
What shall we do, my heart, old shag?

' – You were called home by your mother to her long cold stare
Of ignorance and fright, your father in his whisky-chair
Gazing through the dying embers into smoke-and-oil-filled air;

To the war that dragged on in their living room, that seemed
A drearier affair than the one he'd fought and you had dreamed,
That drove him out each day, tweed-and-twill-uniformed, Brylcreemed

For some respite at the office; while you sought refuge in
Rich-smelling pages, words that raised goose-bumps on your skin –
Poetry, your secret vice! Your still-enervating sin!. . .

The lines I fed to you and your lot set you on your course;
I watched your pennant flying from the south coast to the source
Of the Rhine or Rhône, I listened as you sang yourself hoarse…

But what can you make of England, of her historic wrecks
And of her people fed on lies and lotteries and sex,
The shit-showers of stupidity that rain down on her decks?

This country of ours where nobody is well, as the poet said.'
Then as he skipped away, he twirled an ashplant in his head;
Who'd spent his life in service to the great, ungrateful dead.

~~~

Too late for you to go on board
Trade Winds *wherever she is moored*
And chug upriver, skippered by
Piratical Marie, her eye –
The one without a patch – *intent*
On pubs where you two often went
To huddle over charts together:
Scotch, log-fire, landlubber weather. . .

Where were they, the tall ships of salt-water days? – In irons
In a stench of mud and sewage, the stews-like environs
I knew so well, I heard the calls of South London sirens:

'*Now listen, all you modern tars what draw the mid-day potion,*
Good kids, no doubt, in harbour bars, but blimey, on the ocean:
When stormy winds begin to blow the ship is in great motion. . .

This rocky mid-life passage finds you unprepared,
So many of the old crew gone, while you've been spared –
But not for long, while what's to come leaves you shit-scared!

Years ago it would have been the syphilis that got you,
Or opium, or drink – something that would rot you
From the inside out; or a husband would have shot you…

What's happening is not exactly what you'd hoped or planned.
Look at you – unprized laureate of the prostate gland!
Bid farewell to the shipmates you have lost, to the strand

Where they gather, and set sail – for those fortunate isles
Where the only commuting is in nautical miles,
Where the men are men and the women are all smiles;

For the harbour that awaits you, the words that you must write
In love, in hope, in grief, in gratitude, and in despite,
In a fire of self-forgetting, in the watches of the night.'

Deptford

At closing time:
Conspirators, old salts
Who knew the ropes!
I steered my leaky tub
Past Davy Jones's Vaults
To the Mermaid Club –
Poles like periscopes,
A rising tide of slime…
Looming through the fog
Lurched this sea-dog,
Red-rimmed eye, sweat-
Stained collar, greasy tie;
He chewed a wet cheroot
And necked a grog ration –
Though it was scotch –
To stoke his passion:

Welcome aboard, son,
He roared, *it's your watch!…*
Your grandfather, big man
In Malaya, way back when:
You've seen him
Billow down a sea-stair,
Bully the salt air,
Scan the horizon
For the prize
All true-born Englishmen –
Old-school, born to rule –
Had their eyes on:
The whiff of rubber,
Money, and a stiff
Pink gin. Landlubber,
What if you'd been him?

Miles upriver,
The bastard Tories
Sail on forever;
Propped on pillows
When you were small,
You read their stories,
The Wind in the Willows,
The Cruel Sea...*Poetry?*
A fucking revolution
's what this place needs.
While England bleeds,
Good Queen Lilibet
Pisses on us all.
Her kingdom for a horse –
Get out, for Christ's sake!
Steer a different course!

He stumped off, drunk,
Dragging one sea-leg,
Ahab of the Surrey Docks
Or the Seamen's Mission
In the Old Kent Road...
Beneath my bunk, I'd stowed
A walnut tea-keg:
Heirloom, camouflage,
It kept my powder dry
While I pursued their craft.
Now as I cast off aft
I heard a cough, a croak
From some old soak
Sprawled in the stern –
It was myself, come back
To scold me; *Our royal ship,*

He rasped, *is run to rack*
That was so stout and trim
And some are put unto their shifts
Either to sink or swim. . .
I saw a fusewire snake
Towards a gilded barge;
Saw a match fizz and burn –
It was blown sky-high!

Sailor, Adrift

I knew this path through lanes and alleyways –
The faces in the fog, the salt-scarred, tattooed hands
That groped and grappled, and the taproom blaze,
The glistening skin, the swollen glands;

Sea-road on which I'd often had to navigate
The reef, the rock that should be off the stern
(*The stews of Wapping, Portobello's narrow strait!*)
And learned to expect the unexpected turn

Of the tide…*Those nights*, she said, *those nights are gone* –
The half-familiar woman's voice that flayed me –
So have you learned to keep your life-jacket on?
(I never saw the spiked shot that belayed me.)

You know this path, but can't remember where
It leads, through steep streets, and the crews are lost;
You know that hulk far out in salt-edged air,
The mouldy, sweat-stained bunks on which you tossed. . .

Look at you, still that same suburban
Boy who would not set sail in Gypsy Moth IV
With Sir Francis Chichester, Greenwich to Durban,
But spent your life scavenging the sea-floor!

A jagged lee shore looms. Have you picked up a dose
From that pick-up in your last port of call –
And was that Portobello or Porthcawl?
What does it matter? You were never close. . .

Remember that for one whole night you held me,
Listening to my heart, where you'd dropped anchor;
You're all at sea, you who tasted, smelled me –
Moaning like the sad fog-warning buoy.

To the Lighthouse: Finistère

with Tristan Corbière

Les Triagoz, was it, or La Corbière? –
named for 'the crows' nest'
(though crows have given way
to gulls), not your famous father. Tristan, you knew
the currents, tide-rips, rocks and shoals,
they were in your blood, you, one of the *gens de mer* –
tubercular scarecrow
who gave the citizens a scare
when you lurched through their streets,
bent double: the *Ankou*, collector of souls. . .

Somehow I'd blagged my way on board
as crew –
or was this, not your cutter but my grandfather's, *Spray*?
You clutched the mainsail-, I the jib-sheets,
our arthritic hands like tree-burrs,
both of us coughing. . . Heartbroken, heart-sore,
you could still handle a boat, the *chufere*
and the *fine*, and yourself,
while I, I had your lines by heart,
your sailors' profanities, puns of a race apart. . .

Tristan! You were history. I was high and dry.
Our fathers would have sent us
both to sea, the *carière*
ouverte aux talents – instead you hauled a dinghy inside
your family's summer home-from-home
to sleep in, while I spent forty years
on a berth sheltered from
the brown swirling current of careers.
Now, at twice the age you were when you died,
with half your talent, and nothing put by,

I craved a tot or shot. . . Beyond the bluff,
a perfect storm
brewed down the years in clubs and boardrooms
by those strutting bullies with their word, *perform*,
their piss-taking in the ward-rooms,
the 'guys from finance' and the CEOs,
the ministers without portfolios,
without much else –
was all we had in store;
where were the *Cutty Sark*, the *Compass Rose*,

where were the galleys, carracks and caravels,
the flapping pennants and the furled
sails ruffled by a breeze
from halfway round the world,
the plucky pleasure boats, the little-ship flotillas?
What ice-bound seas,
what 'sad, deserted shore'
were waiting, what hidden shoal
I always found, wherever I made for,
torn flags snapping in a glare of failure at the Pole?

Spray

Now I had almost forgotten the view
From behind, that half-dried seaweed smell,
Smell of something that died long ago in its shell,

They meant nothing to me, they could not hurt
Any more than commonplace memories do:
Of her in that flimsy summer skirt,

Of sitting with her to a plate that was all shells
And rubber, that we both struggled with,
Of the *maitre d'* who laughed like Neptune in a myth,

Of our running through a downpour on the prom
To shelter in a café that could only serve us tea,
Of her padding down the beach to the sea

In a black one-piece, my hand inside it, her *aplomb*. . .
She would not be waiting by the bandstand,
Hair streaming and eyes bright, saying, 'Loser!

I bet you're wondering if I can still be had
For the price of a double at the Grand?
Are you sick or mad? Don't you understand

How much I wanted you, how I prayed you'd die
Calling out for me. . .?' Instead it was my gull-accuser
That swooped to the cast-iron railing with its beak

Wide open, fixed on me an unblinking eye
And regurgitated this: *So you haven't slept!*
There's never been a bunk you haven't crept

Or crawled away from, looking foolish, weak.
Your nights are all bad dreams soaked in remorse,
Your days all lost in longing for what's past

And past repair, for the unknown, uncharted course
In your head. Jesus, could you even raise a mast?
How frail it is, your little craft of. . . Now the shore

Was washed away, was a white ghost net
Of spray – I ploughed on, hunched in a hood
That hid my face like the one I wore

The night we walked out here, a night to forget,
The night I waved goodbye to her for good.
You could lose yourself in that, and drown

Where neither shout nor blurted prayer unlocks
Help from cannonades of air. Go down,
Everything's awash, go down to the rocks.

Shark Song

Sharks patrol the Norfolk Broads,
The playing fields of Eaton Square,
The local geriatric wards.
Blood in the water everywhere,
Frantic thrashing in the shallows,
Flash of fins, and splintered sallows;
A feeding frenzy at All-Hallows,
Wapping Wharf and Shadwell Stair.

And this is good for us! Sink or swim;
If a shark takes an arm and a leg
It's how things are, law of the gym,
Law of the sea. Get out and beg!
At Bank, Hyde Park and Oxford Circus,
Jaws clamped open, hunting workers,
Breeders, brooders, strivers, shirkers,
The chicken and the egg,

Sharks are feeding. How they feed!
More air, more paving stones and mud,
More like us (*do we not bleed?* –
A shark picks up the scent of blood
From leagues away): unlucky losers,
The left-behind, the boozer-users,
Livebait for those cruising bruisers,
Smooth arrivers on the flood.

No-one, fuck! can stop us feeding.
We ate the mines, the mills, and now
The small towns in the hills are bleeding
And everyone to us is chow.
The weak are easy meat; a shark
Will just as breezily take down
The fools who loiter after dark
Outside the Mitre or the Crown.

Our best bet is to get away
To some backwater B&B,
A rain-flecked window and a tray
Of crab-paste sandwiches for tea;
Gin and whisky, those slow killers,
Rows of damp Victorian villas
And the pub, the old Green Pillars –
While they gather out at sea. . .

Feel the fine salt drizzle falling
On the undercliff's red clay,
Hear the gulls like drowned souls calling
To be saved on judgement day;
Feel your fifty years, a cargo
That makes your aching timbers groan;
Sharks have placed under embargo
Everything you called your own.

Free Enterprise

A rich silt
all the way from Zeebrugge
slides across the Astrakhan rug
in the home of Sir Staunchly Sterling.

He sits late,
he has reports to prepare.
He does not see the stain, greyish, thick
as an oil slick, easing its way towards him.

But when sleep
finally comes swirling
like black air, stiff with salt
and the smell of diesel, through his brain,

a clacking fleet
of white, drowned skulls
bobs up the stair, little capsized hulls
that crowd the home of Sir Staunchly Sterling.

Feeder

Basking in the Mayfair afternoon,
the Killer Whale, the male.
Undersea light
filters through the fronds
of sea-grass – urban ferns
and hanging-basket leafage.

He has come to feed,
he lingers, lunches
on small fry and crustaceans
which he crunches, on gilts and bonds,
on something by Jeff Koons
and the woman's cleavage.

There is a need
for gradual overpowering
in his hands, which prod her
here and there, feeling
for the soft spots,
the intimate recesses where

he can deliver hurt –
there is a need for devouring
in his playful excesses,
sea-spurt and sea-squirt!
Such vagaries of appetite,
and only the ocean

with all its teeming zones
to nourish him. . .
Why her stunned face,
why that commotion
in the shallows, that wave
of indignation on the shore? –

Unrest among the bottom-feeders,
clicking of iPhones,
writing of leaders.
You can't fuck with someone's head
in peace, in public, any more.
It's outrageous. It's a bore.

A Night Sail

for Marie Colvin

I dreamt of sailing *Spray*, grandfather Herrick's
pilot cutter, from its berth in an old black-and-white
on the kitchen wall, past the docks, the cranes and derricks,

not to some sluggish oil-rainbowed bight
with pier and prom, in the lee of Gosport or Goring,
not to the wild side of the Isle of Wight

or even a Winslow Homer Nassau mooring
but a secluded cove, where we'd ride at gentle anchor. . .
When I woke, you were still snoring

your smoker's snore; I saw the cliff-face of a super-tanker
and, tied up to starboard, someone's super-yacht,
flying the flag of Panama, or Casablanca –

this was before the crash, not
that the crash would have bothered *him* –
motionless behind its oil-rich haze, its hot

sides gleaming and all its tackle trim;
a super-model, fresh from her shoot on the Ile Ste. Marguerite,
her neat mound cupped in a scrap of scrim,

supine on a sun-deck, inviting him to eat –
A drink first maybe? You choose. . .
The air pulsed with the steady thresh and thrum, the beat

of her super-engines, super-screws,
and suddenly someone had drawn a veil, a pall
of grape-dark clouds over the plaque for La Pérouse.

~~~

Storm-light on the marina, the harbour-wall,
and on the sea beyond. The steady thresh and thrum.
The little pastel boulevards, the palms and all

the quayside bustle and the prosperous hum
of restaurants in that unfashionable resort, the vines and olive groves
inland – a sunburst showed me how far I had come

from London, S.E.1 to the purples, mauves
and deep blacks of that bay, the opalescent blues
and blue-greens of a thousand inlets, creeks and coves

– but *Spray* was gone with grandfather Herrick and his muse
and all that I'd held dear was up for sale,
and it wasn't looking good, for me or La Pérouse.

~~~

You were still snoring. I saw a faded, flapping rust-red sail
and under it, your head propped on sacks of rice
in the bows of a caïque. . . Here I draw a veil,

a veil of tears and old malt over thinking twice
before coming with you across the wine-dark sea to Zuwara,
for I had drunk the milk of paradise,

I did not keep that appointment in Samarra,
I could only lie awake and listen for your whimpers to subside
to snores or read to you from John Grisham, John O'Hara

or John Donne; I did not see the sewer where they died,
the bloated corpses floating downriver, villages laid waste,
the heaps of blackened limbs on each roadside;

how the lives of others were degraded and debased
in camps and market squares, in bare-bulbed basement rooms
at police headquarters, how the nameless and effaced

lingered on the air in airless catacombs;
how the first bones to surface from mass graves
were children's bones, how gas from punctured wombs

alerted those who clawed at rubble, or how a man behaves
who finds his wife and daughter, headless, in the street,
how a man sinks to his knees and moans and raves. . .

~~~

I would have woken you, inviting you to eat,
if I had sailed with you on that caïque
you took from – where? Not the Ile Ste. Marguerite,

not the Isle of Wight – but the flesh was weak,
or I was, and I made some excuse. The old fear,
of falling short, of being found out, of the yellow streak

that runs through me like the streak on the 'beautiful fusilier',
caesiao teres, on the yellowtail or on the gilthead bream,
sparus aurata, that noses through its still-clear

blue-green glaze – further glazed by steam –
on the ancient Persian or Syrian ceramic tile
you picked up in Beirut from a Karim or an Ibrahim

and lugged back for me, that I might sit in style,
in state, under the bathroom shelf
where it sits; that I might look at it and smile

as I think of its weight in your grip, of your contempt for pelf
and perfidy, of your straight dealing and your guts
and have to get a grip on myself

when I recall how you forgave my Ifs and Buts
and brought this back for me, thinking of the bream we ate
in that Lebanese place I sit in till it shuts.

~~~

I sit in and pick at the grilled bream on my plate
and drink the fierce north African rosé, carafe
after carafe, on the evening of our 'date',

year in year out, imagining the chat, the jokes, the chaff
that could not keep those rockets from their target, from the screen-
door of the house you slept in that last night; remembering the gaffe

I made the night we met, and the packed shebeen
we met in, crushed up close on benches, and the reek of *kif*,
of Silk Cut and Gitanes, and all the nights between;

remembering how you almost came to grief
so many times, with your 'I guess they don't make men
like they used to', not in a sudden squall or on a reef

like La Pérouse, but 'in the field', and how again and again
you'd make light of the risks you took,
'on the ground', whether Tamil or Chechen

or Taliban, and how you read me like an open book
when I made my excuses and instead set off –
not on a dhow packed with spices for the *souk*,

not on a fishing smack out of Roscoff
with Tristan Corbière, bound for St. Peter Port,
and not on *Spray*, but on the Eurostar to Paris, *putain, boff*.

~~~

Then south to that unfashionable resort
where I ate a bream and drank a carafe of the local *gris*,
thinking of the risk you ran when you first caught

Gaddafi's eye, when he came on like the Sheik of Araby
in his desert hide-out, and how your straight-talking saw you through;
of that line, *This level reach of blue is not my sea*

and of the storms that broke over you,
the wilder, crueller waves, 'the terror of a child
that is really pure pleasure' which you experienced as crew,

the *splinters and spars and dripping, salty weeds*, and they restyled
as your USP, your 'brand', those buccaneers
whose bounty you became, though you were undefiled;

of the night I was granted the freedom of Algiers
by some PLO big-wigs you conjured from thin air
in a restaurant in Notting Hill – so I'd have to spend years

not writing my Life of Albert
('Our great *Arab* writer') Camus, as you didn't write
your Life of Arafat; of your struggles with that hair,

its dense cloud of curls, rich-brown, and how night after night
you'd started on the second bottle by the time
I turned up, and the 'cascade of butterflies in shafts of light'.

~~~

– In Sri Lanka, that was, where they made you mime
Surrender and lie down, and killed you anyway –
or so you thought, from the pain. Another war-crime

(this one cost you your eye) . . . If we'd sailed from Oyster Bay
to Little Neck, or walked the sands of Zahara
de los Atunes together, or drunk *arak* in Raouché;

if you could have promised, say, a tent in the Sahara,
or Leptis Magna, *al-Khums*, Khoms –
but you kept your appointment, not in Samarra,

not in Baghdad or Basra, or among the piers and proms
of the *vieux port*, and not in Tunis, where you were tailed
for two weeks, but in Homs.

~~~

'*Half-steam ahead by guess and lead, for the sun is mostly veiled…*'
Blue and white sails on the river, but one, a faded rust-red,
was not among them – the dinghy that you sailed.

You held the wheel of *Trade Winds*, aka *African Queen*, instead.
You'd invited me so many times to join you for a cruise,
upriver, down; and now that you were dead

you intimated there was 'no way' I could refuse –
your final offer. You laughed your smoker's laugh
when I climbed aboard, as if to say, What have you to lose,

what have you ever had? Moper, mooncalf,
landlubber, pub-haunter…There was dried blood
on the gunwhales, on the coaming, and down one half

of your lovely, laughter-lined face! With the flood
we drifted upstream, through fast-running bends,
past hollow-eyed dark barges sunk in mud,

past the Ship, the Swan. *The luck on which this life depends*
(you said), *the stats, the stories that we tell, the roar*
of incoming, and the sudden death of friends. . .

Here is the slipway where, when you were four,
you watched your mother slip and almost disappear;
the cemetery full of south-west London men 'lost' in the war.

But all the things that matter happen far from here.
'England expects', the signal sent by sat-phone. . . Not any more.
The ferryman was waiting, back at Chiswick Pier.

Ledbury Road

Two poems in memory of Mick Imlah

1.

'Hardy and Housman lived round here',
You said, slumped in an armchair in your flat.
'Compared to those two, we're small beer –
Hardy and Housman, geniuses crowned here!
No blue plaques for us, who've gone to ground here…
We're pygmies compared to giants like that,
Hardy and Housman, who lived round here',
You said. Slumped. In an armchair. In your flat.

2. (K.F.)

I can't remember, Mick, if 'Ca the yowes'
Was one we listened to together,
Long after closing time, in your small flat
With the almost-derelict sofa, the bows
Of our boat heading into heavy weather,
The cigs, the whisky and the chat
Running out, both of us blind, close to tears
As 'our Kath' sang our longing and our fears…

But you're gone now, and so are they
Who sometime did me seek (*Och no*,
I hear you say, *not that old riff again*)
And I can't make up my mind between
Her Handel Arias with the heartbreaking
'Art thou troubled? Music shall calm thee'
And that song I know can harm me –
Know from the tears, the whisky, the hand that's shaking.

Between (Reprise)

The cat who keeps her distance
And your underhand resistance
A sea of scalding bitter tears.
Between your sly hopes and your fears
Of failure, that lost-in-thought routine,
Passive-aggressive. And, between
The walk of shame, well-dressed, discreet,
And mocking voices on the street:

A barbed-wire fence, a sad-sack guard
Who takes out his already-hard
Equipment, demonstrates its use.
Between the dry slit and the juice
An internet porn site that's free
To those who can afford it, *me*,
A word you like to linger on,
The nub you put your finger on.

Between your pleasure and your pain,
Between Prague's tramways and the train
That brought you here to me, a bar
In Amsterdam or Paris, far
California's rocky coast. . .
Between the thing you wanted most
And what you do not know you want,
A Man who's always there to haunt

Your sleeping and your waking hours,
To devastate you with his powers
Of divination and his knack
Of never giving one word back,
One word of love back. And it sucks.
Between the ebb and flow, a reflux:
Sour tang of coffee, toast, wheatgerm
(Your breakfast) and a gob of sperm.

Between your look of disbelief
And mine of angry, frightened grief,
Between the life I counted on
And blood counts that showed how far gone
The illness was that tied me to
The skill of specialists, the view
That each one takes, the special fear
That all their knowledge and good cheer

Might count for nothing in the end:
My shameful longing for a friend,
Peremptory and violent, raw. . .
Between the kindness that you saw
As deathly, the unsexual touch
You had never valued much –
A need you counted second-best
At best – and that all-giving breast

I'd never known, you'd never known:
A 'tragic view of life', home-grown,
Some gnomic articles of faith
(Not the kind the preacher saith
But a sphinx in rue de Lille);
The *jouissance* you could not feel,
Or would not. That business back
In Santa Cruz. The Law. The Lack.

Between us, tattooed on your hip,
The ideogram that (you let slip)
Meant 'game', the summer dress, blood-red,
I loved you in but which, you said,
'Just isn't *me*'; the plant (bonsai,
Or cactus?) that you had me buy –
From all the richly-stocked Marché
Aux Fleurs one cold, bright Saturday,

You chose it, and it clung to what
It knew, a galvanised steel pot,
A carpet-square of sunlight in
Rue Oberkampf, unwholesome, thin
And wintry, or a dust-filled glare –
Between the likeness you found there,
'Erect' and 'thrusting', and this man
The joke was on: your five-year plan.

Night-swimming, Regent's Park

I was swimming, night-swimming, in the grass.
I was swimming but I was drowning, and I held on to you
As if only you could save me – and it was true,
I was holding on for dear life. But let that pass.

I can feel your mouth on mine, can feel your skin
Burning under me; I can see the midnight park,
Beeches, oaks, horse-chestnuts rustling in
The silver, lake-reflected, moonlit dark.

I can feel your mouth on mine. I can hear
Your laughing words, 'It's just because I'm young',
I can feel the sudden bowel-clutching fear
As I clung and clung.

The stars rang in my head. The heat
That had soaked all day into the grass
Released its scent of yearning and defeat –
My yearning, my defeat. But let that pass.

A siren wailed, *What now What now* but I held on,
Too drunk to wonder where this led
Or if I'd drag you down – then it was gone,
My legs and arms felt heavier, my head. . .

'Because I'm young', you said, and I, I almost drowned,
What with the moon, the trees, the grass
And its scent, you with your scent, all round,
And you in my arms. But let it pass.

Inshore

O the beautiful head of that dutiful daughter
In the prow of the boat that plied between islands,
Between the harbour and the Bay of Silence –
She swam a while then, dripping water
Lay with her head propped on one freckled arm
While the shadow of the parasol grew shorter
And sun-struck village, shuttered square and palm
Trembled like the iced drink I brought her

In its misted glass. . .*You hear the metronome,*
Clicking, as I rocked above you on the beach;
You see the birthmark, little patch of home
Above my tail, by no means out of reach;
The light that bounced off uninterrupted blue
To tremble on the freckled skin you kissed –
You saw it flicker when I turned on you
A distant look, my grey-green eyes like sea-mist!...

Fog closed in, I could make no headway
Against the headwind and the undertow;
In the cracked porthole, the towns of Medway,
Some glittering new-builds, a bungalow,
An office park; on the incoming tide,
Around the boat, I saw them bobbing –
Blue-black, bloated faces, ones who'd died
By falling off their barstools, still stock-jobbing –

And one gasped, *How will you make amends*
For the ancient crab you hooked below the pier,
For the endless rounds that killed your friends,
For your laughable attempt to steer
A dinghy on that puddle in the park?
Who drudge and cark and care for worldly trash,
Among the super-tankers moored your barque,
Among the super-yachts, before the crash?. . .

Up to my balls in bilge-water, bailing
For all I was worth, I heard the Mayday calls
Of the clueless crews who'd gone down, flailing,
In the recent spate of unexpected squalls –
Splintered decks, keels split from stern to stem;
Overboard went compass, lead and oar –
While smiling captains (nothing troubles *them*)
Steamed away to sheltered berths offshore.

Coked-up, fucked-up, we never saw it coming –
Rudderless, we were driftwood on the flood;
Our screens lit green, our hard-drives humming
When the whole bloody issue was covered in mud –
You watched us go for more, the boat at anchor
In the bay, the barbecue's bleeding meat,
The bimbo in the deck-tub in Sri Lanka,
The starved little girl inviting us to eat. . .

I'd steered clear of shit-storms, stayed afloat –
Through luck, not skill; I'd navigated shallows,
I'd never left the shore!. . . My leaking boat
Limped past Gravesend, Greenwich and All-Hallows,
Until by divers courses I had come
On a broad reach to this familiar berth
Where a whiff of Senior Service and bay rum
Announced his shining dome and ample girth:

My grandfather, in the hatchway. *Look here, boy:*
To break your mother's heart, your father's too –
Your childlessness denying her that joy,
Your jumping ship at Dover, when the crew
Were half-seas-over, scuppering his hopes!
Bad blood, some curse. . .was that what you claimed
Prevented you from learning all our ropes,
From putting out to sea? Aren't you ashamed?. . .

I made my way upriver in a daze,
The steering gone, the ensign ripped to shreds,
The log was missing several torn-off days
And an evil backflow filled the heads;
Glistening oil-snakes slithered past the hull
And swirled around the cockpit's unscrubbed boards,
Stained by the droppings of a single gull
Who strafed me: *A long way from the Broads!*,

It croaked. *Your life bobs like a little yacht*
In heavy seas, it veers and bobs and weaves
As if the helmsman were a soak, a sot;
In its wake the wash an empty vessel leaves.
You thought you'd dodged the famous coastal shelf. . .
ENGLAND EXPECTS is the signal that one sends
But your flag flies at half-mast: for yourself,
Or those who loved you, and met watery ends?

Over its vanishing, I draw a veil –
Over the diesel-stench and thrumming screw,
Over the sudden sense that life could fail
To be that richer, riskier thing I knew
Before the years of drift, in the days of sail;
A veil of drizzle on the mud-brown bank
Where nothing was engendered, nothing grew
But scum the tides left as they rose and sank.

Sirens' Song

Remember when you breezed into the Swan,
The Mermaid or the Dove, and swayed
And swaggered like a buccaneer
Who scented plunder, below decks and above?
Remember how the crew
Sat laughing in the stern, how far gone
The ship's complement of women were?

Remember that sharp stink in the heads,
The rocky beds, the calm as you rowed free
And the path *au bord de la mer* −
A thin brown arm around the cliff?
How you might have made a go of it with her
But instead watched all your gear
Go overboard with your learning and your love?

Will you − same old riff − never learn?
That you will not find safe moorings here,
Or at Chiswick Eyot, or anywhere;
That you should expect the unexpected turn
Of the tide that leaves you all at sea,
That some mistakes are final, that too late
Is too late, is spindrift, is thin air?

Poster Girl

M.C.

You were waiting for me in the Underground.
Larger than life, though less lined or scarred
by it, by shrapnel, vodka, nicotine. . .

So much more of you than on the screen
I'd stared at all that day, scrolling through
the jumpy phone-footage till I found

you, yes – but faceless, lying under charred
and pock-marked rubble in your dust-caked jeans,
your blue sweater caked with dust.

The S-buckle on your belt, so I knew it was you. . .
So much more now, and less. I looked hard
at the face, it was the face I loved and took on trust

or took for granted, the sea-green eye alert
for danger, lips parted; and where there'd only been
that shaky picture, pitiful, unjust,

was another you, so clear, and clean,
and alive again, so alive it hurt,
and lost again, in a hiss of doors, a rancid gust.

At Richmond

The gardens are in bloom your mother loved.
A jazz trumpet blares – 'Stormy Weather' –
to a girl spread with her laptop on the grass.
Delinquent for a day, you came
to catch the last of summer on these paths
or the bank grown perilous with out-of-control,
knotted weeds, where your father fished
at weekends, where, midweek, only tourists stroll
and the river-god, Old Father Thames,
cuckoo-spit shining in his beard,
is unfazed by the pleasure-boat's farting horn.

How they clung here by their fingertips
to respectability, slipping each year
a little further down a terrible, almost-sheer
drop into bottomless debt. You, meanwhile,
rose beyond the world of 'bread',
heedless of where yours came from; chose
another music, being free to choose.
At Richmond the river is running for the city;
Though the tall houses on the hill and hotels
In white paint hint of the cliffs and broader sea,
He cannot falter nor alter from his nature. . .

Lines you took to, and took to heart, at fifteen,
your poetic years, when you haunted
the bookshop run by a red-faced,
purse-lipped, cantankerous old queen
who taunted you with how you probably hadn't read
'anything except – who? *Ted Hughes?*'
That stung with its wrongness. A year or so on,
it was the folk-club in the church crypt – another
well-brought-up sensitive with cavalier hair
and songs of consequence-free love
on mattresses in flea-market-furnished attics.

You had your share of that, more than your share.
The bookshop flogs interior design,
the old boy's long dead, like your mother
and father, and the sky's gone dark; gulls drift above
the river, driven by a storm. *That*'s still here,
at least – the pub in which you watched
the 'legendary' Peter Green sip a beer –
he was alone, but you were too shy to speak. . .
Too late now, much too late.
And suddenly you recall her next line:
Lord, neither let falsity my days dissipate.

Salvage

Heroes

Upstairs, I found the box of medals, ribbons, shells –
sorting them, I was in his element, remote
from literature, and my mummy's-boy self.
And here was the Luftwaffe pilot's leather coat
he 'borrowed' from a corpse, its heavy lining flecked
with blood, or maybe *schnapps*. I'd worn it through
my teens – its ripped seams proof of my neglect –
and loved its manly stale-tobacco smells,
its collar I turned up to look sardonic and aloof
as a '40s hero…But these needed sorting too –
the green- and orange-covered Penguins on their shelf,
Conrad, Simenon, Somerset Maugham…
She called from downstairs, 'Mind you keep warm!'
Or 'Supper's ready. Don't you want to watch *Das Boot?*'

Back Numbers

I took home by the sackful from his den,
Picture Post, *Yachting World* and *Minotaur* –
long hours of dreaming at his drawing board
or messing about on that long-sunken boat.
Also *Men Only*s, *Penthouse*s, *Mayfair*s –
not 'airbrushed', these 'models for the girls he sketched',
these purple glossy lips, legs splayed, outstretched: such
gave him solace. But the other lines I wrote
back then, when he died – about my habits, his,
and how none of them waited 'for the artist's touch' –
they return to haunt me now my stares
are met with scowls, and only girls like these
extend an invitation, such as it is,
to back numbers such as me, where no-one sees.

Personal

Tonight we have a game called Bits and Pieces,
in which she hands me some of his old loves
saying she wants me to have them. Silk scarves,
handkerchiefs. A lady's silver hip-flask. Halves
of a plump fob-watch, stamped '1910. Den Haag'.
A slender cigarette-case, too slender for
my flavourless, filtered smokes. I smooth the creases
in a pair of dainty chamois leather gloves. . .
Some of them, *his* mother handed on.
The rest are Shepherd's Bush, Chelsea Arts, pre-war
bohemian and dandyish. Except his fibre dog-tag,
indestructible, 1119681;
and this ring I always thought his wedding-ring
but was, she says, 'for luck. A personal thing.'

Mr Crabtree Goes Fishing

We approached them while a mist still clung to the river –
Eel Pie Island, Cross Deep, Teddington lock, the weir.
He was Mr Crabtree, I was Peter. Though not quite:
he sucked on Players, not one of his pipes, as our floats
bobbed about in the wash made by pleasure boats
and the gin palaces run by advertising men –
it was us and them, the same as it had been for ever.
The morning's 'fragile loveliness', the moment when
my float began to waver, dip and dither,
our trance-like idling on the bank together –
we'd got clean away, to a world of bait-tins, water-tight,
rod-rests, the keepnet filled with little roach or dace. . .
His rods stand unused in my study now, and, here,
his pipes propped on the bookshelf: all in place.

London Irish

My grandmother's 'old boy' worked for a tea-importer
(black bowler, brolly in all weathers, day in day out)
and for Christmas and her birthday brought her
intricately laminated tins of China tea. . .
Fifty years. She'd been widowed at twenty.
Suppers of tongue and new potatoes and stout
and Radio 4, the club, a week in Ireland somewhere
every summer with a spinster sister (did she go first?);
he left a trunk (initialled), a watch that I still wear,
clothes-brush, shaving-brush and bowl, the razor
he did not use to cut his throat. That last time
he was a baby, toothless, in a cot with raised
metal bars, white stubble on his chin like frost. . .
He was always so particular. Now look at him.

Duffel Coat

He saw my fear of water, and was kind,
as he always was, he did not mock or scold me.
Almost the only times that he would hold me –
around my middle, while I kicked my legs behind;
then the brisk rub-down while my lips turned blue.
The towel he wrapped me in was sandpaper-stiff
with salt and sand, I clutched it to myself as if
for burial at sea – not that I yet knew
what that was – while I staggered drunkenly
back and forwards in the shallows' yellow froth.
My fear of water! I wouldn't sleep under sailcloth,
shrug his duffel coat on and lace my mug of tea
with brandy on the bridge; but when I swung the lead
for years, and spouted bilge, what did he see instead?

Clipper

Masts, deckhouses, hatches all to scale, perfect
in every detail – cleats and ports and balsa pulley-blocks:
this two-foot three-master he carved and modelled,
varnished, painted on solitary nights,
stolen weekend afternoons. When he died,
she was given to me in trust. Now she lies furred
and blanketed with dust, the cotton rigging
in disarray, broken spars suspended from the threads.
The damage is even worse when you go aft. . .
No-one has dropped her, or dropped anything on her.
No-one has come near her. But forty years
have done their work, as patient as he was,
undoing all this craft. . . New addictions now, new wars,
and ghost ships moored in deserted high-rise docks!

Smoke

All autumn, the chafe and jar
of nuclear war
                    Robert Lowell, 'Fall 1961'

My father, who'd had
about as much as he could take
by '44, and still woke
swearing at flies
and soaked in sweat,

read the *Telegraph*
in dread and disbelief
over his first cigarette,
narrowing his eyes
against the scroll of smoke. . .

Only half-awake,
dreaming a bitter,
penitential cup
of coffee, we squint
at a screen instead of print,

swipe through
and see plump child-men
jerked by the strings
of Twitter,
their sad posturings

that could turn us to smoke
before we can even laugh.
A father's no shield
for his child – nor
a husband for his wife. . .

Nothing now is a joke,
nothing is so mad or bad
it cannot happen.
To that 'well-meaning guy'
outside a club in Paddington

who saw her lighting up
and told her she should stop,
Marie just said:
'I promise you,
this isn't how I'll die.'

In Sailor's Locker

His vow

The life I spent so lavishly
   Before we met
Seems one long night, in memory,
   Of sea-fever and sea fret –
Which led me here, to you, to this:
   Our haven below decks.
You anchored me, I you, with a kiss
   (Though the coast is strewn with wrecks).

His epitaph

Over the long day of his memorial affair,
Over all that was said in Hangover Square
And later, I draw a veil: a veil
Of tears and songs that still ring true, that never fail
Now that the only real life, the life elsewhere,
And everything we loved, is up for sale. . .

After that I draw a veil, of course,
Over nights in New York, at the White Horse,
Or the Ship, or one of a hundred bars
Where the whisky failed to grip, on leaving which –
One foot in the gutter, and an eye on the stars –
He was always falling face-down in a ditch.

Player's Navy

I work to make my flat proof against the winters,
My flat roof, my skylights and window-frames,
Unhelped by him, who gave our claims the slip. . .
When I kneel to strip the rough planks of my flooring,
Sanding when the soiled, soaked rag snags on splinters,
My head swims with the shining decks of twelve, thirteen;
With white spirit and the whiff of coiled rope. I see him
Straighten up to light another Player's Navy Cut,
Snap the lighter shut and smooth his moustache-ends
With the back of his hand. I tell myself we were friends
As I reel home after drinking all night in The Ship,
Make my window-latches fast, batten down the hatches
Of my skylights then keel over in the wrack
Of oily rags, the reek of the years that I want back
And listen to the room creak and strain at its mooring.

John Knox Laughton in West Kensington

A Liverpool master-mariner's son
and Cambridge mathematics graduate;
Instructor RN at twenty-three,
'one of the finest in the Service', who showed
'courage under fire' in the Second China War,
at thirty-six he came ashore
to teach at the Royal Naval College. . .
'Reduced' at fifty-five, he embarked
on the second of his careers,
as Professor of Modern History
at King's London – in his 'spare' time
contributing more than 900 lives
to Leslie Stephen's *DNB*,
all 'naval worthies', an 'unofficial History of the Navy'
(the only one he could write, given
the 'problem of access to archives');
plus notices (sixty-odd in forty years)
for the *Edinburgh Review*.

Produced a pot-boiling *Nelson*,
the two-volume *Memoirs & Letters of Henry Reeve*. . .

Just thinking of his work-rate makes me weary,
but to men of his generation
it would have been nothing new,
and he could even be reckoned
a failure: no *magnum opus*,
no grand synthesis or defining theory –
tireless networker, correspondent,
he founded the Navy Records Society
and devoted himself to
a 'sure and accurate record', knowledge
'as to how a seafaring people became a nation'.

~~~

At that same age, fifty-five,
a widowed father of five
he remarried, and brought his new wife
here: a house in one of the brand-new terraces
a fellow-Scot had 'had a mind' to build,
west of smarter Holland Park –
street names, Caithness, Maclise, Masbro, Sinclair,
that helped him feel at home, perhaps,
among the clerks and brokers,
army officers (retd.; Bombay, Madras)
and lady piano teachers. . . A house they filled
with five more children, a cook,
Bridget Kieley, nursery maid,
Ellen Varnell, and housemaid,
Margaret Connell. . .

                    By the turn
of the century they had moved twice –
to Barnet, then Wimbledon, where they stayed.
He abhorred alcohol, the week's
'inevitable drunk' at Christmas.
In his eighties, his son Leonard's neglect
of his duties as Secretary of the NRS
gave him much cause for concern:
'Either the boy is from home, or he is off his head'.
He died at eighty-five.
Almost nothing more is known –
surrounded by so many lives,
he left no Life of his own.

~~~

The house is four flats now, and I
live on the top, the 'nursery' floor, and sit
to my work in the attic room
I call my study – a ten-by-ten-foot box
with the delicate outermost twigs of a garden lime
tapping at the windowpane,
a net of lime-tinted light and shade
falling on the knots and clean-scrubbed grain
of the floorboards' Victorian pine; where
one morning, coming into it
straight from sleep, I sat drowsily
and heard, instead
of the usual barking dogs and single blackbird,
a stifled sob, someone quietly whispering:
Margaret and Ellen, talking of home,
each in her narrow bed,
blankets drawn up to the chin. . .
                                        First light
slanted over the roofs, through thin
curtains, and ash fell softly
in the cold grate. Clocks
ticked, downstairs. The master and everyone
would be stirring, there were fires to be lit.

Blue Days (Sailor's Return)

Mon coeur las des ciels et des mers. . . (Henri de Régnier)

I know this path through cypresses, an olive-grove,
Know it from a time before the 'holiday village'
Brought Dutch and Brits and Germans to this cove
To grill themselves, drink and rape and pillage;
I took the path repeatedly and waved away
The pine-needle cobwebs from my face, to see
Between the cypresses that blue glimpse of the bay –
The little bay that opens out invitingly,

The little beach where locals take their ease.
I was in love with everything I saw:
The olive-leaves that shimmied in the slightest breeze,
The donkey groaning under its hump of straw;
The little bar, the dry clicking noises made
By worry beads in the fingers of old men
Who sat to *tavli* at wooden tables in the shade,
The fried fish and the wine full of resin, then;

With the opalescent blue-greens of the water
And with the mermaid who swam in on the tide,
Who parted salt-wet lips as her mother taught her
And slicked herself before she slid me inside –
I can see her grey-green eyes, their fleck like foam
On a choppy sea; the birthmark like wet sand
Above her tail, the tiny patch of home,
Her home, that I traced with my free hand.

Out in the bay the toy sloop rode at anchor
(I remember how those eyes opened wide
As she rocked above me), at the harbourside
The water-cargo flowed from a low-lying tanker
As fishing boats spilled their gleaming catch
(And I remember everything that was said
Over our last drink beneath a vine-leaf thatch,
When she told me *she was leaving, love was dead. . .*)

~~~

How can you stand it, to come back to
This sun-scoured attic room, a whiff
Of mildew and a sun-bleached powdery bloom

On its walls − the little window holds a view
Of sea, of masts and dazzling sails by Dufy
And you can taste the salt on her skin,

You take the sheet in one hand, the helm in the other
As your skiff skims lightly over the water,
You gybe and tack, gybe and tack, white spume,

Salt spray − the sail billows and the stern
Comes through the wind, too late, the boom
Comes over, the keel like a shark's fin

Breaks the surface, you are in − when I say 'you'
I mean: an old salt at the point of no return,
And that dutiful daughter, the freckled crew...

Later, on your berth, she throws a plump brown arm
Around you, you are in love, the sea is calm
And the heart-shaped stone you found to weight

The tablecloth sits neatly in your palm.
(When I say 'you' I am not talking straight,
I mean someone who was I; all the rest is true).

~~~

Five years since I came here to heal my heart,
My heart grown weary of the storm-grey skies,
The storm-darkened seas, all sown with lies
And stale pretence: the vanity of art....
I healed it lying in a hammock with
Lives of the Great Navigators: de Gama,
Magellan, Drake and Hawkins, bold as myth;
Discovery and conquest, all that drama.

The road not taken!. . . I haunted dockside bars
And bore the sweat-stained lascars' crooked smiles,
Their rum-soaked stories of the Fortunate Isles,
The whine of ocarinas and guitars
In hope someone would offer me a passage to
The land I knew existed, far beyond
My silted harbours – the dreams of a boy who
Sailed his model boat across the village pond.

I came here to heal my heart, twice-broken
By her to whom I would not give it back
To break again, by her whom I watched pack
And leave with tears unshed and words unspoken.
I healed it lying in a hammock reading
The sad, bad, drunken seer Houellebecqs's
Anathema on breeding and non-breeding
Humans, pleasure-punishing themselves with sex.

(And we did quite a bit of that, my love:
Across the captain's table, in the heads
Where you took it like a man, and in so many beds
Where gently, underneath me or above,
You worked yourself up to the point of no return;
You fucked with skill – *Dear heart, how like you this?*
And there were many moves I had to learn –
Such as the spine-tickle and the shoulder-kiss...)

I drank myself to sleep, then woke and wept
For the hot nights, the jasmine-heavy air,
The *shush* of waves from the balcony where
We'd stretched ourselves on cool stone tiles, and slept;
For the nights she wore her fraying silk
And wriggled out of it, for the hieroglyph
Of love she made, pouring honey on goat's milk.
I lay in darkness and a stiff breeze, stiff.

~~~

You had said goodbye to them, the quayside places,
The days on beaches, nights in bars, the wine,
The hours you'd watched light fall on their faces

Like a benediction – girls who smiled from doors.
You had watched them growing smaller, the terraced hills
Studded with hotels and villas, the bedraggled palms,

The laughing heiresses with sailing skills,
Bare-breasted, bare-assed, who took you in their skinny arms
For a night or two then waved you off before

They ordered breakfast in some harbourside café.
The dutiful daughter who saw you come to grief
On the rocks and shoals around the Château d'If.

You found a flat stone, heart-shaped, to keep it all
From flying away…This narrow bunk, jagged lee-shore
And mayday call are yours. (When I say 'yours' I mean mine.)

~~~

I came alone, to this place of healing –
Its flow of waterlight, unbroken blue,
Its many scents – in search of something true,
Heart's-ease, because *I had not right feeling*
towards women – and because I had steered
Too recklessly into those latitudes
Where pack-ice jammed it round, and storm-birds jeered
At what I thought to salvage, what platitudes

Of the jasmine-scented breezes, gentle waves,
Of the storm-swell and the steamers' wake, the surge,
Of her warm wetness when she felt the urge,
Of so many crews gone to their graves;
Of the longing in her foam-flecked eyes,
Of salt and seaweed on the tongue, going south,
Of the salt-wet happiness between her thighs
And the artistry in her downturned mouth;

Of the day she straddled me in the long grass
Above the harbour, of her faraway look
As I stroked and fingered her armpits, her arse –
She knew it all, she read me like a book,
Not the tide-tables or the book of charts
But a manual called The Mermaid's Dark Arts,
The art of taking and breaking a man's will
So that a man feeds but is hungry still. . .

I lay and worked on my unhappiness
While the sun went down behind a great humped whale
And the fishermen's little gaff-rigged sail
Grew smaller, the disturbance less and less
As their engine pulled a single wrinkling thread
In the flat silk of the sea. . . I saw her laugh
Her wide, white laugh, her beautiful blonde head
Bobbing, while I took my photograph,

Above the waters of the dark blue bay –
The Bay of Silence; that dutiful daughter,
I saw her tanned arms spread out on the water
As she waded on to the beach where I lay,
I tasted salt on the nipple-puckered cloth
Of her one-piece – but that taste could not last:
My mouth filled with a tide of yellow froth,
Brackish, bitter, the taste of ports long past.

~~~

In a room behind a bar off the Canebière
You meet the skipper for a final heart-to-heart –
A stale smell that takes the wind out of your sails,

The floor almost underwater, the nearby *slap, slap*
At the harbour wall, a smoke-filled circle of light on the ceiling
From a single kerosene lamp; sea-dogs sat on rope-bales

Round a bottle, one of them dealing
From a greasy pack of cards. You study the chart
By sea-light – sharp little glints from the oil-black quiff

And shiny-silver suit of a shark who lolls
With that dutiful daughter in his lap,
His hand skimming lightly over, now a stiff

Nipple, now a dazzling thigh. 'He sailed here in a skiff
From Casablanca – she's one of his molls. Mud in your eye.'
(Here's looking at you – when I say 'you'…)

~~~

I have come back to this place of healing,
The blue translucent haze of sea and sky,
In search, this time, of whatever does not die...
Fortress, harbour wall, the village kneeling
At the mountain's foot, in penance or in prayer;
The pelican that squats on its cistern perch
And cries out to the petrol-laced, salt air
That the sea has gone to live inside the church.

Unhappy bird, not lost but not at home,
You flap bedraggled wings above our wake
For scraps that never come, and for their sake
Waddle the shoreline, the flotsam-littered foam:
I treasure you as much as if you were
The albatross itself, and in you, see
What I have been these ten years without her –
Unreconciled, unappeasable, unfree.

You and that lizard in a patch of shade
Are my companions now, my shipmates while
This voyage lasts, and in a little while
You'll show me myself, and what I've made:
Of this narrow bunk where love might have grown,
The rough night-crossings and the morning calm,
The scallop-shell ashtray, the heart-shaped stone
I found, that now sits neatly in my palm;

Of those giant, stranded, bristling storks, the palms
That stand in salt glitter, in the petrol-glare
Of dockside streets, and of the terraces
With olive groves that shield the heiresses
Of shipping fortunes in their pools, their air
Of freedom as they move about the deck –
Brown skins, a flash of white...Of her freckled arms
Outstretched towards me from the sunken wreck.

~~~

When I say 'you' I mean you, the woman who
Sat with me in that bistrot on the corner –
We'll always have Paris, you said –

For lunch after lunch in sunlight; where I'd wait
And think of a time, *mon coeur las des ciels et des mers*
When I would live in a room off the Canebière

Without love, behind a dazzling cigarette,
Seek out that bar where it is always evening
And tell anyone who'd listen how, *with his sea-green hair*

Charles Baudelaire dragged himself on a leash
Through the streets of Paris, and sang, so long ago,
'Somewhere beyond…Là-bas', as the barman stands

Forever calling time. . . . Time heavy on my hands,
I would sit in an old trenchcoat, stylishly out of date,
And drink to you – a salt sea grieving

In landlocked, long complaint – then steer dead ahead
Through a thin drizzle towards the lights of yachts
Tied up in the harbour, I would always be leaving

But not on one of them, my decks awash,
The crew long gone and I the only mourner
Of the lost years I have not drowned yet.

Notes and Acknowledgements

'Salt-water Days': Like many young boys of my generation I was glamorized by the wartime exploits of the Royal Navy as depicted in films such as *The Cruel Sea* and *Battle of the River Plate*. After a couple of years at my nautical school, the glamour of the sea-going life had begun to wear off. Among the staff I encountered a particular kind of sea-dog, crackling with anger and disaffection; also some more 'artistic' souls who seemed slightly out of place.

'Deptford': One of the masters, who combined both those elements in his make-up (ex-Merchant Marine, and an ardent admirer of Shelley's political poems), features in 'Deptford', along with my mother's father, who died when I was two. The latter was born in 1900; conservative in outlook, resourceful, a boat-owner at his happiest on water, he didn't exactly serve the Empire, but made a living from it. On the outbreak of the Second World War he joined the Royal Naval Volunteer Reserve. Deptford, on the River Thames in south-east London, was once synonymous with the English seafaring spirit and the shore-life of sailors. (Christopher Marlowe was killed there, while Joseph Conrad's Marlow has passed it countless times on his way up or downriver: 'Hunters for gold or pursuers of fame, they all had gone out on that stream'.) I lived on the border of Deptford and its smarter neighbour Royal Greenwich in 1979-80. In 2012, the royal barge *Gloriana*, built to celebrate the Diamond Jubilee of HM Queen Elizabeth II, was docked just upriver from Deptford at Greenland Pier, where the Queen officially named her.

'A Night Sail', 'Sirens' Song', 'Poster Girl', 'Smoke': Marie Colvin was an American-born foreign correspondent, employed for most of her working life by *The Sunday Times* and based in London. Her reports from the world's conflict zones (especially the Middle East), which emphasised the suffering of civilians in war, received many awards; Muammar Gaddafi and Yasser Arafat were among her admirers, while her courage in the face of danger was celebrated far beyond the political or journalistic worlds. She had several narrow escapes in the pursuit of her calling, but was killed in a rocket attack in Homs, Syria, when the house in which she and other journalists had established a makeshift media centre was targeted by the forces of Bashar Al-Assad. A French photographer, Rémi Ochlik, was also killed in the attack. *In Extremis: The life of war correspondent Marie Colvin*, by Lindsey Hilsum, was published in 2018; one of its epigraphs is Dorothy Parker's poem 'Fair Weather', from which I have borrowed a line and some phrases (in italics) in the sixth section of 'A Night Sail'. (The first line of the final section is from Kipling's 'Rhyme of the Three Sealers'.) *A Private War*, a feature film based on Colvin's life, was released in the UK the following year, with Rosamund Pike in the lead role; large posters advertising it appeared in London Underground stations, showing Pike/Colvin in a characteristic pose. Colvin's last home was beside the Thames at Chiswick, and in her spare time she loved sailing.

'Between (Reprise)', 'a sphinx in rue de Lille': the French psychoanalyst and Surrealist Jacques Lacan, whose riddling, reverential exegeses of Freud's works have had a profound impact on psychoanalytical and literary thought. 'The Law. The Lack': key terms (and concepts) in Lacan's theory of the Unconscious.

'At Richmond': The title and the italicised lines are borrowed from a poem by Anne Ridler. The Richmond in question is also on the Thames, in south-west London; the poem makes a kind of pair with 'Deptford' (see above).

I'd like to thank Jo Evans, John Kinsella, Gwendoline Riley, and the late Emma Tennant for their advice and encouragement; also the editors or publishers of the following, in which some of these poems, or earlier versions of them, first appeared: *Blue Days: The Sailor's Return* (with images by William Pownall, London, 2012), *Five Poems* (Thame, 2015), *Greenheart* (London, 1990), *The Guardian*, *Harm* (London, 1994), *Jubilee Lines: 60 poets for 60 years* (London, 2012), *Liberties*, *The London Review of Books*, *Marine* (with John Kinsella, London, 2015), *New Walk*, *Paper-Money Lyrics* (London and Toronto, 2014), *The Spectator*, *Tidemarks* (Nottingham and Leicester, 2018).

ALAN JENKINS was born in 1955, and has lived in London for most of his life. He has worked as an editor, reviewer and teacher in England, Europe and the United States, and published several volumes of poetry, among them the Forward Prize-winning *Harm* (1994), *A Shorter Life* (2005), *Revenants* (2013) and *Marine* (a collaboration with John Kinsella, 2015). New Walk Editions published his chapbook *Tidemarks* in 2018.